Birthe Beigel

GO FOR IT!

Teacher's Resource Book

A1

Hueber Verlag

GO FOR IT! A1
Teacher's Resource Book

Quellenverzeichnis
P. 29: shopping cart © Thinkstock/Hemera/Vadim Shulepnikov
P. 31: onions © fotolia/Tomboy2290; bread roll © Thinkstock/iStock/kgfoto; sausages © Thinkstock/iStock/winterling; garlic © Thinkstock/iStock/Luis Carlos Jiménez del Río; eggs © iStock/YinYang; potatoes © Thinkstock/iStock/ruzanna; mushrooms © fotolia/gudrun; jam © Thinkstock/iStock/Denira777; vegetables © Thinkstock/iStock/Serghei Velusceac; cheese © fotolia/sumnersgraphicsinc
P. 35: coat © Thinkstock/iStock/Suljo; blouse © iStock/lypnyk2; boots © Thinkstock/iStock/ronstik; scarf © iStock/hatman12; dress © Thinkstock/iStock/Cherkas; jeans © fotolia/Alexandra Karamyshev; shirt © iStock/ARSELA; suit © iStock/timhughes; skirt © Thinkstock/iStock; shoes © Thinkstock/iStock/MaleWitch
P. 43: illustrations © Hueber Verlag, München/Virginia Azañedo

3. 2. 1. | Die letzten Ziffern
2019 18 17 16 15 | bezeichnen Zahl und Jahr des Druckes.
Alle Drucke dieser Auflage können, da unverändert, nebeneinander benutzt werden.
1. Auflage

Umschlaggestaltung: Sieveking • Agentur für Kommunikation, München
Gestaltung und Satz: Sieveking • Agentur für Kommunikation, München
Verlagsredaktion: Nina Lötsch, Hueber Verlag, München
Druck und Bindung: Kessler Druck + Medien GmbH & Co. KG, Bobingen
Printed in Germany
ISBN 978-3-19-032938-0

Art. 530_18248_001_01

Contents

	Activity	Use	Focus	Page
Unit 1	**Hi, I'm Peter**			
	1 Country battleships in pairs; game	classroom activity 7	Alphabet; Numbers 1–20; Country names; *Is it …?; Yes, it is. / No, it isn't.*	6
	2 An international party whole class; mingling	classroom activity 8	Greetings; Asking about personal details; *Can you spell that, please?*	9
Unit 2	**That's a big family!**			
	1 Meet the family in groups / pairs; information gap	classroom activity 5	Talking about families; Possessive determiners; Possessive *-'s*	12
	2 Family pairs in groups; game	classroom activity 6	Lexical field: family members; Numbers 1–100; *Do you have …?; How old is …?*	14
Unit 3	**That's a cool job!**			
	1 What's the time? in groups; game	classroom activity 4	Asking and saying the time	16
	2 I love my job in pairs; information gap	classroom activity 6	Talking about routines; Present simple: questions, positive statements	18
Unit 4	**I like mud running**			
	1 Free-time activities in groups; game	classroom activity 3	Agreeing / disagreeing; *(don't) like + -ing; can / can't*	20
	2 The 'I like you' chant whole class; jazz chant	classroom activity 5	Object pronouns	22
Unit 5	**We had a great time!**			
	1 All of us were at a pub whole class; mingling	classroom activity 2	Past simple of *to be*	24
	2 Sam's trip whole class; mingling	classroom activity 4	Past simple: questions, irregular verbs; Days of the week *(revision)*	26
Unit 6	**Enjoy your meal!**			
	1 Shopping for food in pairs; information gap	classroom activity 2	*Is / Are there any …?; Yes, there is / are.; No, there isn't / aren't.*	28
	2 Flashcards: "food" whole class / pairs / groups; various activities	classroom activity 4	Lexical field: food	30

	Activity	Use	Focus	Page
Unit 7	**It's a bargain!**			
	1 I need a gift in pairs; role play	classroom activity 4	Shopping; Lexical field: clothes and souvenirs	**32**
	2 How much are the boots? in pairs; information gap	classroom activity 5	Asking for and understanding prices; *How much is / are...?; It's / They are ...*	**34**
Unit 8	**A great holiday!**			
	1 Special days in pairs; information gap	classroom activity 3	Saying and understanding the date; Special days around the world	**36**
	2 What am I doing? whole class; miming	classroom activity 4	Present continuous: positive statements	**38**
Unit 9	**How do we get there?**			
	1 Where's the post office? in pairs; information gap	classroom activity 4	Prepositions of place; Places in a town / city; *Where's ...?*	**40**
	2 Show me the way in pairs; peer dictation	classroom activity 5	Giving directions; imperative	**42**
Unit 10	**I don't feel very well**			
	1 Health crossword puzzle in groups / pairs; crossword puzzle and information gap	classroom activity 2	Lexical field: body and health	**44**
	2 Healthy food for a happy life in pairs; information gap	classroom activity 4	*How much...?; How many...?; How often...?*	**46**
Unit 11	**Let's go out!**			
	1 At a ticket office in pairs; role play	classroom activity 3	Asking for information about an event; *can; have to*	**48**
	2 Are you free on Friday? whole class; mingling	classroom activity 4	Making arrangements; Present continuous for fixed plans and arrangements	**51**
Unit 12	**I'm learning English**			
	1 International neighbours in pairs; puzzle and information gap	classroom activity 2	Talking about personal information and language skills	**53**
	2 Multiple Intelligences in pairs; interview and quiz	classroom activity 4	Theory of Multiple Intelligences (H. Gardner); *like + -ing; Are you good at...?*	**55**

This resource book is aimed at teachers working with *Go for it! A1* and teaching basic English to learners with little or no prior knowledge of the language. It provides material for 24 communicative classroom activities. In these activities, learners produce the newly acquired language structures in different contexts – this helps them to memorize and eventually use them fluently.

There are two activities for each coursebook unit. Each activity corresponds to a specific exercise; it can be carried out directly after the coursebook exercise for consolidation, or later on for revision.

Using the Teacher's Resource Book

There is one page of teacher's notes for each classroom activity: these are comprehensive step-by-step instructions on how to prepare and carry out the activities. They also provide additional ideas on how you can vary or extend an activity according to your students' needs and abilities.

There are various types of activities with different classroom interaction patterns: students interact in pairs, in groups or with the whole class in order to play games, do quizzes, info gap activities, etc. The focus of the activities is on speaking, but the other skills (listening, reading, writing) are practised as well.

Go for it! A1 meets the requirements of level A1 of the CEFR (Common European Framework of Reference for Languages) – in the same way, the activities in this resource book are designed to reflect the communicative situations of the CEFR. Students focus on the corresponding lexical fields, areas of functional language and/or specific grammatical points, and revise them in a light and entertaining way.

To select the appropriate classroom activity for your lesson, look at the table of contents: It shows the corresponding coursebook exercise, the language focus, the type of activity and the classroom interaction pattern. The teacher's notes provide additional information about the activity, such as its approximate duration (since this is dependent on many factors, the times given in the book can only provide a general guideline to help classroom time management).

Further resources for teachers

The *Go for it! A1 Teacher's Guide* (978 3 19-022938-3) provides comprehensive information on working with *Go for it! A1* in class. You can find further teaching material on the *Go for it!* web site under www.hueber.de/go-for-it.

We hope that these resources will help you to add variety to your lessons with *Go or it!* and to respond to the heterogeneity of your student groups.

Your *Go for it!* team

Use Unit 1, after classroom activity 7	**Activity** in pairs; game
Duration 20 mins.	**Focus** Alphabet; Numbers 1–20; Country names; *Is it …?; Yes, it is. / No, it isn't.*

Preparation

Make one copy of the two worksheets for each pair of students.

Procedure

1. Tell students they will play a guessing game which is similar to the game "Schiffe versenken" (Battleships), but instead of ships, they will have to find the names of countries in their partner's grid.

2. Make pairs (Student A and Student B) and hand out the worksheets.

3. Students ask each other about the coordinates in their grids: Student A begins and says a letter and a number from the grid titled "My partner's field", e.g., *W15*. Student B answers by saying the corresponding letter (e.g., *R*) in their grid (titled "My field") or by saying *No, sorry* if there's no letter in their grid. If Student B answers with a letter, Student A notes it down and goes on asking about other coordinates. If Student B answers with *No, sorry*, it's their turn to ask.

4. Once students have enough letters to guess a country name that's hidden in the grid they may ask their partner, e.g., *Is it England?* Their partner answers with *Yes, it is* or *No it isn't*. Write examples of the question and answer phrases on the board for students as a reference.

5. Students play the game until they have found all the country names in their partner's grid (there are five in each grid). After the activity, students compare their worksheets to check for correct spelling.

Extension

Pairs who finish quickly can write city names from Unit 1 in their grids and continue playing.

Student A

■ *W15?*
● *R.*

■ *Q14?*
● *No, sorry.*

My field:

	A	B	C	D	E	F	G	H	I	J	K	L	M	
1					I	R	E	L	A	N	D			1
2							N							2
3							G			S				3
4							L			C				4
5		C	A	N	A	D	A			O				5
6							N			T				6
7							D			L				7
8										A				8
9	S	W	I	T	Z	E	R	L	A	N	D			9
10										D				10
	A	B	C	D	E	F	G	H	I	J	K	L	M	

My partner's field:

	N	O	P	Q	R	S	T	U	V	W	X	Y	Z	
11														11
12														12
13														13
14														14
15														15
16														16
17														17
18														18
19														19
20														20
	N	O	P	Q	R	S	T	U	V	W	X	Y	Z	

Student B

- *D9?*
- *T.*

- *F7?*
- *No, sorry.*

My field:

	N	O	P	Q	R	S	T	U	V	W	X	Y	Z	
11				A	U	S	T	R	I	A				11
12					S					U				12
13	G	E	R	M	A	N	Y			S				13
14										T				14
15								R		R				15
16								U		A				16
17								S		L				17
18								S		I				18
19								I		A				19
20								A						20
	N	O	P	Q	R	S	T	U	V	W	X	Y	Z	

My partner's field:

	A	B	C	D	E	F	G	H	I	J	K	L	M	
1														1
2														2
3														3
4														4
5														5
6														6
7														7
8														8
9														9
10														10
	A	B	C	D	E	F	G	H	I	J	K	L	M	

Use	Activity
Unit 1, after classroom activity 8	whole class; mingling
Duration	**Focus**
25 mins.	Greetings; Asking about personal details; *Can you spell that, please?*

Preparation

Make one copy of the first worksheet and cut out the individual 'identity cards'. (You can make an extra copy of the worksheet to refer to as key.) Each student will receive one identity card. Make one copy of the second worksheet for each student in your class.

Procedure

1. Copy the information about 'Shirley Miller', a guest at an international party, on the board (see boardscript below). Elicit a question for each category (*name, country,* etc.). Write the questions on the board as a reference for students.

Name: Shirley Miller	What's your (first) name / surname?
Country: USA	Where are you from?
City: Seattle	Where in the USA are you from?
Phone number: 001 206478281	What's your phone number?
Email address: s_miller@boeing.com	What's your email address?
	Can you spell that, please?

2. Model a dialogue with a confident student. Use the questions on the board. Illustrate the use of *Can you spell that, please?* for clarification.

3. Hand out the second worksheet and one identity card to each student. Tell students to imagine they're at an international party and get to know people from all over the world. They have some information about the people at the party, but some other information is missing. They should use the questions on the board to ask for the missing information.

4. Students get up and talk to as many people as possible. They ask for the information that's missing on the second worksheet and write it down.

5. After about 15 minutes, compare answers in class: Ask students to introduce a person to the class, for example: *This is Bill. He's from the USA.* Ask follow-up questions like: *What's Bill's address / phone number?,* etc.

Extension

Students can extend their class list from classroom activity 5b by adding the categories *country, city,* and *email address* to it and asking their classmates about them.

Name: Ingvar Andersson **Country:** Sweden **City:** Uppsala **Phone number:** 0046 206478281 **Email address:** i.andersson@ikea.se 1	**Name:** Herman Amberger **Country:** Switzerland **City:** Berne **Phone number:** 0041 569257 **Email address:** hiking.amberger@freesurf.ch 2	**Name:** Bill Banting **Country:** USA **City:** Miami **Phone number:** 001 3057889878 **Email address:** b.banting@silverado.com 3
Name: Eva de Marke **Country:** Belgium **City:** Brussels **Phone number:** 0032 2771645 **Email address:** eva_marke@eurounion.bl 4	**Name:** Juan Juarez **Country:** Spain **City:** Barcelona **Phone number:** 0034 93721596 **Email address:** donjuan@simyo.es 5	**Name:** Cassandra Graziano-Calabrese **Country:** Italy **City:** Palermo **Phone number:** 0039 1445557 **Email address:** pastapronto@lamamma.it 6
Name: Agata Kowalski **Country:** Poland **City:** Krakow **Phone number:** 0048 12691340 **Email address:** agata.kow@email.cz 7	**Name:** Teresa Lechner **Country:** Austria **City:** Vienna **Phone number:** 0043 22672910 **Email address:** tessa@waltz_school.at 8	**Name:** Alain Leclerk **Country:** France **City:** Paris **Phone number:** 0033 14683499 **Email address:** office@alainleclerk.fr 9
Name: Lore Leyh **Country:** Denmark **City:** Copenhagen **Phone number:** 0045 3124590 **Email address:** svenja_mermaid@tdc.dk 10	**Name:** Agnetha Lindström **Country:** Sweden **City:** Stockholm **Phone number:** 0046 8128964 **Email address:** ag_Lindstroem89@telenor.se 11	**Name:** Jamie MacDuncan **Country:** Scotland **City:** Glasgow **Phone number:** 0044 141 452963 **Email address:** jmd_1964@whiskix.co.uk 12
Name: Manuela Michaelis **Country:** Germany **City:** Munich **Phone number:** 0049 89354167 **Email address:** manus_stuebchen@web.de 13	**Name:** Akiko Montezuma **Country:** Japan **City:** Tokyo **Phone number:** 0081 3111568 **Email address:** Akiko_cato2@excite.co.jp 14	**Name:** Massimo Paulo **Country:** Italy **City:** Rome **Phone number:** 0039 6759904 **Email address:** papa_paulo@silencio.it 15
Name: Andrea Schmidt **Country:** Germany **City:** Dresden **Phone number:** 0049 3515609607 **Email address:** andi.schmidt78@gmx.de 16	**Name:** Holly Skole **Country:** Ireland **City:** Dublin **Phone number:** 00353 1342225 **Email address:** holly.s@island.co.uk 17	**Name:** Henry Temple **Country:** England **City:** Liverpool **Phone number:** 0044 13144101 **Email address:** templerunner@yahoo.co.uk 18

First Name	Surname	Country	City	Phone Number	Email address
Ingvar	Andersson	Sweden			i.andersson@ikea.se
Herman	Amberger		Berne	0041 569257	
Bill			Miami	001 305788988	b.banting@ silverado.com
Eva	de Marke	Belgium		0032 2771645	
Juan			Barcelona	0034 93721596	donjuan@simyo.es
	Graziano-Calabrese	Italy	Palermo	0039 1445557	
	Kowalski	Poland	Krakow	0048 12691340	
Teresa		Austria		0043 22672910	tessa@ waltz_school.at
Alain	Leclerk	France	Paris		
Lore		Denmark	Copenhagen	0045 3124590	
Agnetha	Lindström			0046 8128964	ag_Lindstroem89@ telenor.se
	MacDuncan	Scotland	Glasgow		
	Michaelis	Germany		0049 89354167	manus_stuebchen@ web.de
	Montezuma	Japan	Tokyo		Akiko_cato2@ excite.co.jp
Massimo		Italy	Rome		
	Schmidt	Germany		0049 3515609607	andi.schmidt78@ gmx.de
Holly	Skole		Dublin	00353 1342225	
	Temple	England	Liverpool		

Use Unit 2, after classroom activity 5	**Activity** in groups / pairs; information gap
Duration 30 mins.	**Focus** Talking about families; Possessive determiners; Possessive -*'s*

Preparation

Make one copy of the worksheet for each student in your class. Cut up as indicated. Make two more copies and complete the family tree for Group A on one of them, the family tree for Group B on the other one (refer to the key below).

Procedure

1. Divide your class into two groups (Group A and Group B). Tell students they are going to read about two different families and fill in their family trees. Hand out the upper worksheet halves with the family trees on them. Hand out one reading text ("Abbey's family" and "Bill's family") to each member of the respective group (A/B).

2. Students read through the texts in groups and complete the corresponding family trees on their worksheets. Walk around and offer help if necessary. When both groups have finished, hand out the completed family trees that you have prepared to the respective group (A/B). Students can now check if they have filled in the names correctly.

3. Tell students to put their texts away. Then make pairs (with a student from Group A and one from Group B). Students describe the family tree on their worksheet to their partner, starting with, e.g., *Abbey's husband's name is Bob*, or *Bill's parents are Eliza and Carl*. Their partner listens and fills in the names in the empty family tree on their worksheet. After they have finished, students compare the family trees on their worksheets (they should look the same).

Extension

Students can write true or false sentences about the family trees then read them to a partner. Their partner answers *True* or *False*, and corrects the false statements. For example: *Bob is Brian's cousin*. Answer: *False. Bob is Brian's brother-in-law.*

Variation

Weaker students can look at the reading text as a reference while exchanging the information about the family trees.

Key

Group A (Abbey's Family):

(from left to right) *first generation:* Dave; Leslie; Linda; *second generation:* Anna; Brian; Bob; Abbey; Fiona; Fred; Felix; *third generation:* Jane; Mary; Frederic

Group B (Bill's Family):

(from left to right) *first generation:* Eliza; Carl; *second generation:* Hanna; Stephanie; Bill; Laura; Max; Claudia; *third generation:* Nick; Josie; Rose; Julie; Emma

Group A

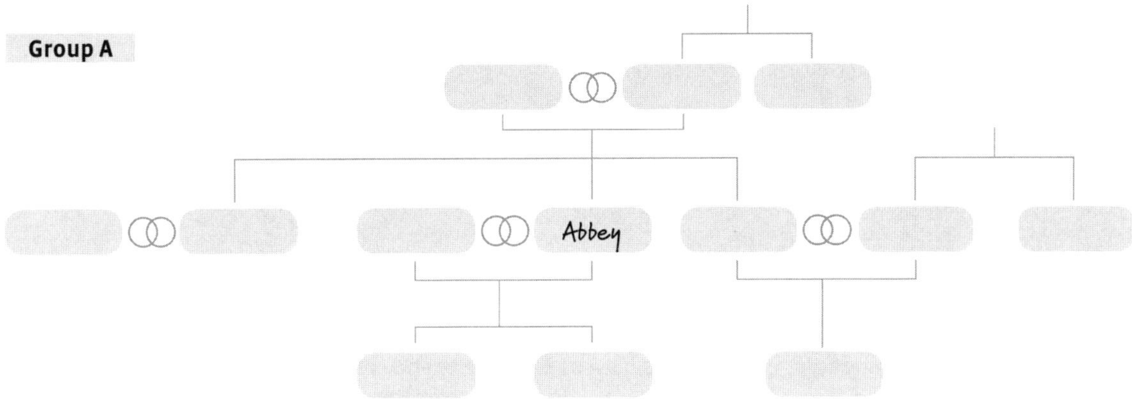

Group B

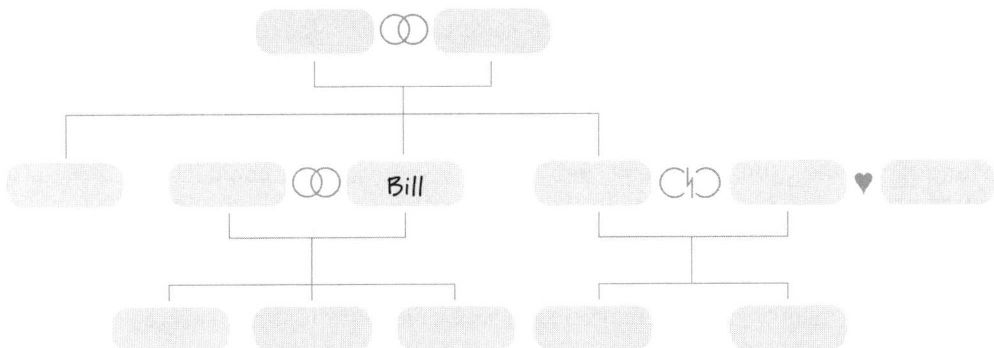

Abbey's family (Group A)

Hey, I'm Abbey. My husband's name is Bob. We have twin daughters. Their names are Jane and Mary. My brother is Brian. His wife's name is Anna. They have no children. My sister is Fiona. She is married. Her husband's name is Fred. Fred has a brother, Felix. Felix is single. Jane's and Mary's cousin is Frederic. Our children's grandmother and grandfather are Dave and Leslie. They are my parents. My mother has a sister. Her name is Linda.

Bill's family (Group B)

Hey, I'm Bill. My parents are Eliza and Carl. I have two sisters, Hanna and Laura. My sister Hanna is single. My sister Laura is divorced. She and her ex-husband, Max, have two girls. Their names are Julie and Emma. Max has a new girlfriend, Claudia. My wife's name is Stephanie. We have three children: Nick, Josie and Rose.

Use	Activity
Unit 2, after classroom activity 6	in groups; game
Duration	**Focus**
25 mins.	Lexical field: family members; Numbers 1–100; *Do you have …?; How old is …?*

Preparation

Make one copy the worksheet for each group of (3, 4 or 5) students and cut it up as indicated.

Procedure

1. Divide your class into groups of 3, 4 or 5 students (depending on class size). Hand out a set of cards to each group (remove two identical cards from the set for groups of 3 students). Tell students to shuffle them well and then deal out six cards (groups of 3), five cards (groups of 4) or four cards (groups of 5) to each member of the group.
2. Before your students start playing, write the questions (*Do you have …?, How old is he/ she …?*) and answers (*Yes, I do. / No, I don't., He's / She's … years old*) on the board for students as a reference. Explain to students that the aim of the game is to collect pairs of identical cards by asking these questions to the other members of their group.
3. Player A chooses one of the cards on their hand. They ask one student from their group about the family member on it, for example: *Do you have a niece?* If the student asked (Player B) doesn't have a card that says *niece*, they say *No, I don't*, and it's the next student's turn to ask. If Player B does have a card saying *niece*, they answer with *Yes, I do*, and A goes on to ask, *How old is she?* Player B has to answer with the information on their card, for example *She's 23 years old.* If the family member on A's card has the same age, B has to give their card to A. Then it's the next student's turn to ask.
4. While your students are playing, walk around class, listen in and help if necessary. The student with the most pairs of identical cards wins the game.

Variation

This game can be played with different types of questions and answers. After the final *Go for it!* task in Unit 2, for example, students could make their own set of cards with family members and information about *pets, (number of) children, marital status*, etc.
Prepare 20 empty cards for this (by folding up sheets of paper several times and cutting along the resulting folds). Students write a family member on four cards. Then they add information which should be exactly the same on each pair of two cards. Students have to use additional questions and answers in order to find pairs, e. g., *Does (your uncle) have a cat / children? – Yes, (he) does. / No, (he) doesn't*, or *Is (your sister) married? – Yes, (she) is. / No, (she) isn't.*

niece 23 years old	niece 23 years old	niece 5 years old	niece 5 years old
younger sister 28 years old	younger sister 28 years old	younger sister 43 years old	younger sister 43 years old
nephew 13 years old	nephew 13 years old	nephew 30 years old	nephew 30 years old
aunt 86 years old	aunt 86 years old	aunt 48 years old	aunt 48 years old
cousin 53 years old	cousin 53 years old	cousin 35 years old	cousin 35 years old

Use Unit 3, after classroom activity 4	**Activity** in groups; game
Duration 20 mins.	**Focus** Asking and saying the time

Preparation

Make one copy of the worksheet for each group of students (3–4 students per group). Cut up as indicated (you will have a set of 20 dominoes). You may want to laminate the cards or glue them on cardboard for future use.

Procedure

1. Students play a game of dominoes matching numbers with the corresponding spoken expressions.
2. Divide your class into groups of 3–4 students (depending on class size) and give each group a set of dominoes. Ask students to shuffle the dominoes, deal out four dominoes to each student in the group and leave the rest on a pile in the middle of the table, face down.
3. Explain the rules of the game: Player A puts down a domino face up in the middle of the table and says *What's the time?* A's left-hand neighbour has to put down a domino that matches the time stated on either side of the domino. He or she has to say the matching time correctly (for example, *It's four o'clock*). Then it's their turn to put down a domino and ask their left-hand neighbour *What's the time?*, and so on. If a student cannot put down a matching domino, they say *Pass!*, and take a card from the top of the pile. The winner is the first student who doesn't have any dominoes left.
4. Start the game. During the game, circulate and monitor.

Extension

If students enjoyed the game you can use it again after classroom activity 6 in Unit 3 to practise talking about daily routines: When a player puts down a domino, they ask their left-hand neighbour a question about their routine, using one of the times written on the domino, e.g., *What do you normally do at four o'clock?* Their neighbour puts down a matching domino (if possible) and makes a statement, e.g., *I normally finish work at four o'clock*. Then they ask the next student a question with the time stated on the other side of their domino, and so on.

17:50	quarter past ten	22:15	ten to eight
07:50	half past seven	19:30	twenty past twelve
12:20	four o'clock	16:00	two thirty
14:30	twenty-five past three	15:25	quarter to five
16:45	five past six	18:05	twenty-five to nine
20:35	five to eleven	10:55	one o'clock
13:00	half past five	17:30	quarter past two
14:15	twenty to four	3:40	ten to three
14:50	eight o'clock	08:00	quarter to eleven
22:45	twenty-five to twelve	11:35	ten to six

Use Unit 3, after classroom activity 6	**Activity** in pairs; information gap
Duration 15 mins.	**Focus** Talking about routines; Present simple: questions, positive statements

Preparation

Make one copy of the worksheet for each pair of students. Cut up as indicated. Prepare one copy of each text with the questions underneath already completed for students to check (refer to the key below).

Procedure

1. Students read a text about a woman who loves her job, and ask each other questions about it to complete the missing information. Divide the class into two groups (Group A and Group B). Hand out a worksheet half (Student A/Student B) to each member of the respective group. Tell students both groups have the same text, but with different pieces of information missing.
2. Students read through the text carefully then complete the questions below the text with their group. The question beginnings and endings are already written on their worksheets. Allow enough time for this. Circulate and offer help if needed.
3. Make sure the questions on your students' worksheets are correct (for example by handing out the worksheets you have prepared as key).
4. Make pairs (with one student from Group A and one from Group B each). Students now ask each other the questions they have prepared in order to complete the text. Remind your students to answer in complete sentences (e.g., *She gets up at six o'clock*, not just *six o'clock*).
5. Start the activity. Circulate and monitor. When students have finished, give them time to compare their texts with their partner to ensure that the answers and the spelling are correct.

Extension

As homework, students can write a similar text about a person they know well.

Variation

You can ask strong students to write questions about the missing pieces of information without looking at the prompts below the text. Students could also formulate their questions spontaneously to ask for the missing information.

Key

Student A: (1) What's her name? **(2)** What does she do? **(3)** When does she start work? **(4)** When does she have lunch? **(5)** What does she do in the afternoon?

Student B: (1) What's her boyfriend's name? **(2)** Where does she work? **(3)** When does she get up? **(4)** When does she finish work? **(5)** When does she go to bed?

Student A

Her name is **(1)** ______________ and Robert's her boyfriend. She's a **(2)** ______________ and she loves her job. It's really interesting. She works in a big city hotel. She normally starts work at **(3)** ______________ so she gets up at 5 a.m. She works in the morning and has lunch at about **(4)** ______________. She finishes work at 2.30 p.m. but she doesn't normally go home then. She often **(5)** ______________ in the afternoon and she sometimes ______________. Her job is hard so she's tired in the evening and she normally goes to bed at 10 p.m.

1. What ________ her name?
2. What ________ ________ do?
3. When ________ ________ start work?
4. When ________ ________ have lunch?
5. What ________ ________ do in the afternoon?

✂ -

Student B

Her name is Rita and **(1)** ______________'s her boyfriend. She's a chef and she loves her job. It's really interesting. She works in **(2)** ______________. She normally starts work at 6.30 a.m. so she gets up at **(3)** ______________. She works in the morning and has lunch at about 11.30 a.m. She finishes work at **(4)** ______________ but she doesn't normally go home then. She often goes shopping in the afternoon and she sometimes meets Robert. Her job is hard so she's tired in the evening and she normally goes to bed at **(5)** ______________.

1. What ________ her boyfriend's name?
2. Where ________ ________ work?
3. When ________ ________ get up?
4. When ________ ________ finish work?
5. When ________ ________ go to bed?

Use Unit 4, after classroom activity 3	**Activity** in groups; game
Duration 15 mins.	**Focus** Agreeing / disagreeing; *(don't) like + -ing; can / can't*

Preparation

Copy the worksheet twice for each group of (3, 4 or 5) students. Cut up as indicated. Keep the two sets of 20 cards neatly separated: One is for students to deal out, the other one is the pile.

Procedure

1. Write a free-time activity on the board (e.g., *swimming*). Elicit statements about the activity, such as *I like swimming* or *I can't swim*. Highlight the *-ing* form in the former and the base form in the latter sentence.

2. Remind students how they can agree or disagree to statements like the ones on the board (see boardscript). This was introduced in classroom activity 2d.

I like swimming. ☺ Me too. ☹ Really? I don't like swimming.	I can't swim. ☺ Me neither. ☹ Really? I can swim.

3. Practise the dialogues on the board with a confident student. Point out the intonation in the answers by exaggerating the emphasis on *Really?* and the (modal) verb. If students master this, the conversation during the game will be more fluent and fun.

4. Explain that students will speak dialogues like these while playing a game of cards. Then make groups of 3, 4 or 5 students (depending on class size).

5. Hand out two sets of cards to each group (for groups of 3 students, remove the same two cards from each set). One set is the pile, the other, identical, set is for students to deal out: They deal out either six cards (group of three), five cards (group of four), or four cards (group of five) to each member of the group.

6. The first student takes a card from the pile and silently reads the activity on it. If they have the same activity card on their hand, they put the card face down under the pile and take another card from the top. If they don't have the same activity card, they put the card face up on the table and make a statement with *I can('t)* ... or *I (don't) like* ... that is true for them about the activity. They have to decide whether to use the modal verb or *like + -ing*, since the verb on the card is either in the base form or ends in *-ing*.

7. The student who has the same activity card puts it down on the table and replies to the statement, agreeing (*Me too., Me neither.*) or disagreeing (*Really? I like ... / I can ...*, etc.). Again, they should answer in a way that's true for them. Then they take a new card from the pile and start the next mini dialogue.

8. The first student to put down all of his or her cards wins. Walk around and monitor while your students are playing.

Extension

Ask students to report one surprising thing they found out, e.g., *Peter can't swim.*

swimming	play snooker	bake	playing football
play the violin	ski	reading	gardening
play chess	playing tennis	playing computer games	doing yoga
doing nothing	going for a walk	cook	play the guitar
watching TV	dancing	having a drink with friends	swim

Use Unit 4, after classroom activity 5	Activity whole class; jazz chant
Duration 10 mins.	**Focus** Object pronouns

Preparation

Make one copy of the worksheet for each student in your class.

Procedure

1. Revise the personal pronouns and the object pronouns with your students, for example by writing them on bigger cardboard, spread them out on a table and ask students to match each personal pronoun with the respective object pronoun. Make sure to keep the pronouns in order (1st, 2nd, 3rd person singular, 1st person plural, and so on).
2. Hand out the worksheets. In pairs, students fill in the missing pronouns. Tell them to look at the list on top of the worksheet. They should use the pronoun that reciprocates the action (e.g., *She likes us.* ⟷ *We like her*).
3. Read out the jazz chant in class so that students can check their answers. Read at natural speed so they can hear the intonation and the rhythm of each line. Students could mark the stressed word in each line (it's always the last). You can also clap the rhythm of each line.
4. Divide your class into two groups (Group A and Group B). They should stand on opposite sides of the classroom facing each other. Start speaking the first line with Group A, then signal Group B to answer and speak along with them too. You can accompany each line with a gesture pointing out who likes who.
5. When you've gone through the whole chant once, repeat it. This time, Group B starts. You could change the tone of the chant: Tell students to speak in happy, bored, sleepy, etc. voices. Remember, jazz chants are supposed to be fun! Keep the atmosphere light, and try to always make sure students join in chanting.

Extension

Students can write their own jazz chants and practise them in class. They can use verbs like *see, go/dance with, tell, ...,* or any other verb followed by an object pronoun.

Variation

Make this a pair work activity: After step 3, students could speak the chant in pairs instead of getting up and speaking it in groups.

Key

I like *you*! – You like *me*!; You like *him*! – He likes *you*!; He likes *her*! – She likes *him*!; She likes *us*! – We like *her*!; We like *you*! – You like *us*!; They like *you*! – You like *them*!

him you her them us

Group A		Group B
I like you!	⇄	You like me!
You like him!	⇄	He likes ______________!
He likes her!	⇄	She likes ______________!
She likes us!	⇄	We like ______________!
We like you!	⇄	You like ______________!
They like you!	⇄	You like ______________!

Use Unit 5, after classroom activity 2	**Activity** whole class; mingling
Duration 20 mins.	**Focus** Past simple of *to be*

Preparation

Make one copy of the worksheet and cut up as indicated. For more than ten students, make a second copy of the worksheet and hand out the same card to more than one student.

Procedure

1. Write a statement about the class on the board, e.g., *All of us were at a yoga class last week*. Be sure to include *last* as this may be new for your students. Ask individual students: *Were you at a yoga class last week?* and write the question on the board. Help students with the short answer if they only answer with *yes* or *no*. Add ticks and crosses next to your statement: a tick each time a student answers *Yes, I was*, and a cross for each *No, I wasn't*.

2. Tell students if the statement on the board is true or false for the class. Tell students they are going to verify similar statements by asking questions like the one on the board.

3. Hand out one of the prepared cards to each student. Students read the statement on their card and think of the question they have to ask to find out if it is true or false. Then they get up, walk around and ask their question to the other students. If they hear a positive answer, they put a tick under *Yes, I was*; for a negative answer, they put a cross under *No, I wasn't*.

4. Give a clear signal for students to start. Monitor carefully especially at the beginning of this stage to see if students ask the correct question. If not, help them individually.

5. After they have spoken to everybody in class, students sit down again. Focus their attention back to the board. Count the ticks you made and write a true statement, e.g., *3 of us were at a yoga class last week* (if you have counted three ticks). Then count the crosses and write another true statement, e.g., *4 of us weren't at a yoga class last week*.

6. Ask students to look at their cards and count the ticks and crosses they've made. They can then write down similar statements about the class and report them back to class.

Variation

If you have fewer than six students in your class, you can copy the whole worksheet for each student and make this a pair activity. Students then won't try to find out what's true for the class as a whole, but what's true for their partner. In the reporting stage, they make sentences about what they and their partner have in common, for example *Susan and I were at a concert last week*, or *Bob and I weren't at a pub on Saturday evening*.

True or false? **All of us were at a birthday party on Saturday.**	True or false? **All of us were at home at 7 o'clock on Monday evening.**
✓ Yes, I was. ✗ No, I wasn't.	✓ Yes, I was. ✗ No, I wasn't.
True or false? **All of us were at work at 8 o'clock on Monday morning.**	True or false? **All of us were out with friends on Friday night.**
✓ Yes, I was. ✗ No, I wasn't.	✓ Yes, I was. ✗ No, I wasn't.
True or false? **All of us were at a concert last week.**	True or false? **All of us were at a funfair last weekend.**
✓ Yes, I was. ✗ No, I wasn't.	✓ Yes, I was. ✗ No, I wasn't.
True or false? **All of us were at a pub on Saturday evening.**	True or false? **All of us were in Italy last summer.**
✓ Yes, I was. ✗ No, I wasn't.	✓ Yes, I was. ✗ No, I wasn't.
True or false? **All of us were in bed at 10 o'clock on Sunday morning.**	True or false? **All of us were in bed at 11 o'clock last night.**
✓ Yes, I was. ✗ No, I wasn't.	✓ Yes, I was. ✗ No, I wasn't.

Use	Activity
Unit 5, after classroom activity 4	whole class; mingling
Duration	**Focus**
20 mins.	Past simple: questions, irregular verbs; Days of the week *(revision)*

Preparation

Make one copy of the worksheet for each student and cut it in two halves. You need to cut up the lower half of the worksheet once for each seven students in your class (twice if you have fourteen students, and so on). In classes with less than seven students cut up the lower half once and give more than one card to each student.

Procedure

1. Students find out details about Sam's trip to a big European city. Ask students where they think Sam went and what he did on his trip. Write "On Monday, Sam ..." on the board. Elicit possible endings for the sentence and write them on the board. Highlight the simple past form of the verbs.
2. Elicit the question to the phrase on the board *(What did Sam do on Monday?)*. Write it on the board above the possible answers. Practise the question with different weekdays and remind students how to say they don't know the answer (*Sorry, I don't know.*)
3. Give the upper half of the worksheet to each student, as well as a card with a weekday and an activity on it. Ask students to add the information from their card to their worksheet (using the correct *past simple* form of the verb).
4. Start the activity. Students walk around in class and ask other students *What did Sam do on ...?* They should write the answer on their worksheet. After they have completed all the sentences on their worksheet, they can sit down again.
5. During the activity, monitor and listen carefully. You may want to note down common errors.
6. Compare solutions in class. If necessary, include a follow-up error correction phase.

Extension

In class or as homework, students could write similar sentences about a trip they went on, following the model on the worksheet. If you compare the texts in class, encourage confident students to report about the trip without looking at their notes.

What did Sam do on ...?
On Monday, Sam ______________________.
On Tuesday, he ______________________.
On Wednesday, he ______________________.
On Thursday, he ______________________.
On Friday, he ______________________.
On Saturday, he ______________________.
On Sunday, he ______________________.

Monday go to Rome	**Tuesday** do a city tour	**Wednesday** see the Sistine Chapel	**Thursday** go shopping for shoes
Friday buy postcards and souvenirs	**Saturday** have dinner at a very good pizzeria	**Sunday** go home	

Use Unit 6, after classroom activity 2	**Activity** in pairs; information gap
Duration 15 mins.	**Focus** *Is / Are there any …?; Yes, there is / are.;* *No, there isn't / aren't.*

Preparation

Make one copy of the worksheet for each pair of students in your class. Cut up as indicated.

Procedure

1. To warm students up for the information gap activity, brainstorm some food items that you can buy in a supermarket. They could write the objects on the board and you could add any other items you need for the activity.

2. Introduce the word "shopping trolley" by showing the pictures on the worksheet (or by drawing a shopping trolley on the board).

3. Tell students they are going to play a quiz game and find out what their partner has in their shopping trolley. Elicit and write the questions and answers they need for this on the board as a reference during the activity:

Is there any … in your shopping trolley? ☺ Yes, there is. ☹ No, there isn't.	Are there any … in your shopping trolley? ☺ Yes, there are. ☹ No, there aren't.

4. Make pairs (Student A and Student B) and hand out the worksheets. Tell students to look at the shopping trolleys on their worksheet. They should ask each other the questions on the board to find out what's in their partner's shopping trolley. They can use the objects you've brainstormed at the beginning of the activity. They should answer their partner's questions according to what's in the trolley on the left-hand side of their worksheet. They have to find six items and write them into the empty trolley.

5. Walk around, monitor and help if necessary. Note down common errors or mistakes for the error-correction stage.

6. When students have found the six items in their partner's trolley, they can compare their worksheets to check for spelling.

Extension

Students who finish early can add more items from the brainstorming phase, or other items you can buy at a supermarket, to their shopping trolley and ask each other about it.

Student A

My shopping trolley

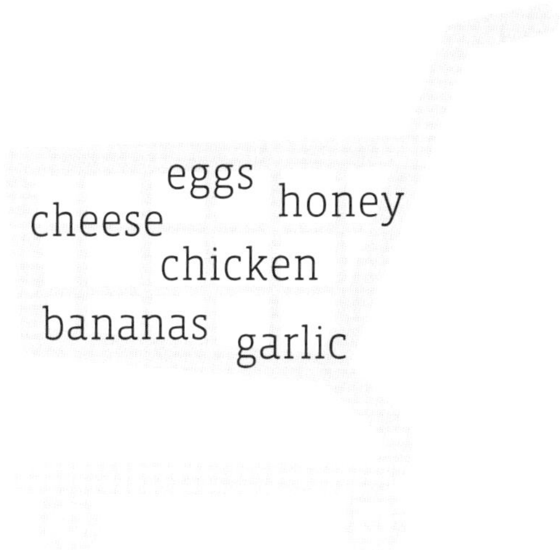

My partner's shopping trolley

Student B

My shopping trolley

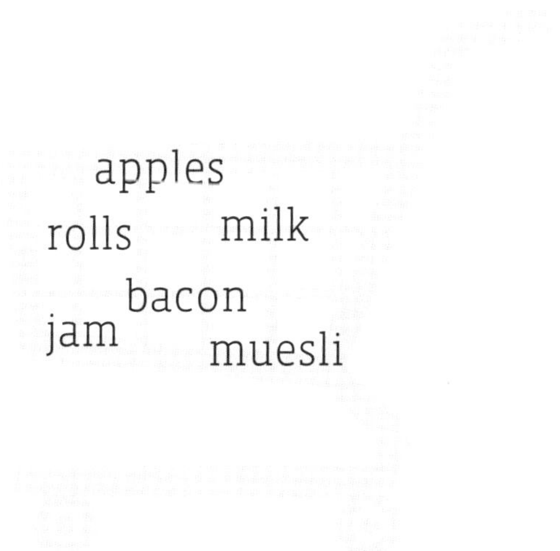

My partner's shopping trolley

Use Unit 6, before or after classroom activity 4	**Activity** whole class / pairs / groups; various activities
Duration 10–15 mins. for each activity	**Focus** Lexical field: food

Preparation

Make a copy of the worksheet. Depending on the kind of activity you are planning for your lesson, cut out each card individually or cut out a word/picture combination to fold in the middle.

Ideas how to use the flashcards

Introducing new lexical items (individual word cards and picture cards)
Show the picture card, say the word and let students repeat. Stop after every fifth card and repeat the most difficult words by holding up the card again and letting students repeat the word. Pay attention to pronunciation and drill the respective word if necessary. After students have memorized most of the words, hand out the word cards to the students, put the picture cards face up on the table and let students match the word cards with the picture cards.

Pelmanism / a memory training game (individual word cards and picture cards)
After you have introduced the lexical field, students can play a game of pelmanism in small groups. Hand out a set of word cards and a set of picture cards to each group. Students put all the cards face down on the table in a maze, and then take turns to turn around two cards. They try to find as many matching picture and word cards as possible.

Sort out! (individual cards or combined word/picture cards)
Revision activity: Put the picture cards on a table and ask students to sort the pictures into categories of their choice. After that, students can present their ideas to the class (in their mother tongue). Ask them why they chose those categories.

Using the lexical items (combined word/picture cards)
You can use the flashcards in a quick and fun speaking activity to help your students practise the language in a multi-learner style way: Hand one word/picture card to each student in your class. Tell students to mingle and ask other students questions that include the lexical item on their flashcard, for example: *Do you like* (item on flashcard)*?* or *When did you last eat* (item on flashcard)*?*, etc., or simply ask for a translation: *What's this in English, please?* (showing the picture side of the card).

	onions		bread roll
	sausages	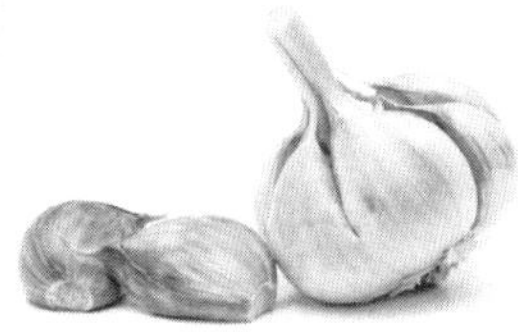	garlic
	eggs		potatoes
	mushrooms		jam
	vegetables		cheese

Use Unit 7, after classroom activity 4	**Activity** in pairs; role play
Duration 20 mins.	**Focus** Shopping; Lexical field: clothes and souvenirs

Preparation

Make one copy of the worksheet for each pair of students and cut it up as indicated. Prepare a few extra copies of the worksheet that you don't cut up. You can give them to students to check if their dialogue is in the correct order.

Procedure

1. Tell students they are going to prepare and role-play a dialogue between a shopping assistant and a client who wants to buy a gift. Make pairs and give one cut-up dialogue to each pair. Students could start by sorting the paper strips into two categories: shop assistant and customer. (With less confident students you may want to check if they have sorted the sentences correctly before going on.) They can then put the dialogue in the right order.
2. After students have finished, you can give them the uncut worksheets you have prepared so they can check if their dialogue is correct. Two voluntary students read the dialogue for the whole class.
3. After this, focus students' attention on the underlined words and expressions – they can be changed in the dialogue. Ask students what other words they can think of, e.g., "I need a gift for my *husband*" (instead of *best friend*). Have students write down some ideas on how to change the dialogue.
4. Students then practise the dialogue in pairs with their variations. Encourage them to react to the changes their partner suggests by changing their replies accordingly. Students should then change roles and speak the dialogue again. At this stage, it is ok if the dialogue changes quite a bit. Students may want to try out the language they have learned in Unit 7.
5. Monitor closely and make some notes for a brief error-correction stage. At the end, each pair can read their dialogue in class.

Extension

Confident students who enjoy practising can cover the dialogue and speak it as freely as they can.

Hello! Can I help you?

Hello! Yes, I need a gift for my best friend.
It's his birthday tomorrow.

That's nice. How about a New York T-shirt?
We have it in black, blue and red.

Ooh, the blue one's really nice! How much is it?

It's €25.75.

OK, I'd like a T-shirt then. Do you have any key rings?

Yes, we do. Look at these.

Ooh, they are really nice. How much are they?

The big ones are €15.50 and the small ones are €7.25.

Hmm ... the big ones are nicer. I'd like two.
Can I pay by credit card?

Yes, of course. We accept Mastercard and Visa.

Thanks for your help!

You're welcome.

Use Unit 7, after classroom activity 5	Activity in pairs; information gap
Duration 10 mins.	**Focus** Asking for and understanding prices; *How much is / are ...?; It's / They are ...*

Preparation

Make one copy of the worksheet for each pair of students in your class and cut it in two halves. Keep one copy of the worksheet that you don't cut up for yourself as a key.

Procedure

1. Draw a sketch of a pullover on the board and ask students what it is. Add a price tag to your drawing but don't write a price. Elicit the *question How much is the pullover?*, and write it on the board.

2. Next, draw a pair of socks with a price tag on the board and elicit the question *How much are the socks?* Highlight *are* and the plural *-s* so that students pay attention to the correct question form during the activity.

3. Get students to ask you about the price of the pullover and the pair of socks. Answer and write your answer on the board, e.g., *It's £89.90* (below the pullover) and *They're £6.50* (below the pair of socks). Then write the price in the empty price tag. Make sure students understand that the currency symbol is written before the figures, e.g., £6.50, but that we say *six pounds fifty*, or *six fifty*.

4. Make pairs (Student A and Student B) and hand out the worksheets. Tell students that each student has only half of the price tags filled in. The other half is missing. The information is on their partner's worksheet. They need to ask each other questions in order to find out what each item costs.

5. Give students a moment to look at their worksheets in order to get ready to ask the first question. Then start the activity. After students have finished they compare their worksheet with their partner to check if they have filled in the prices correctly.

Student A

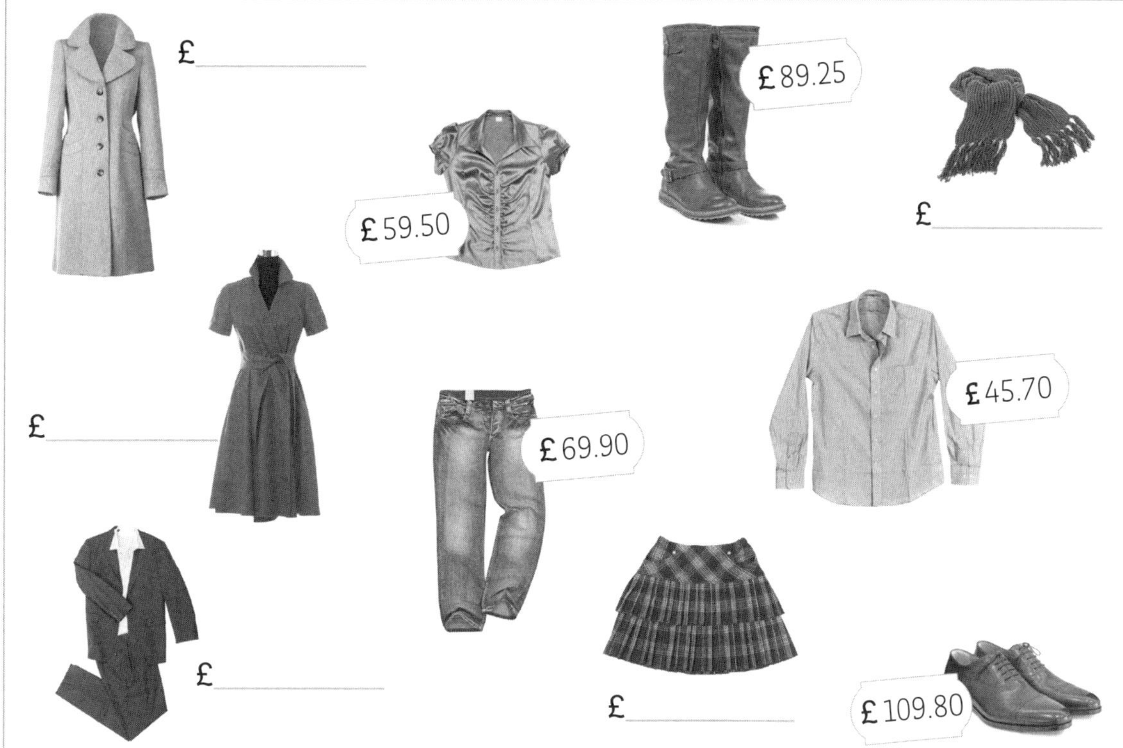

✂ -

Student B

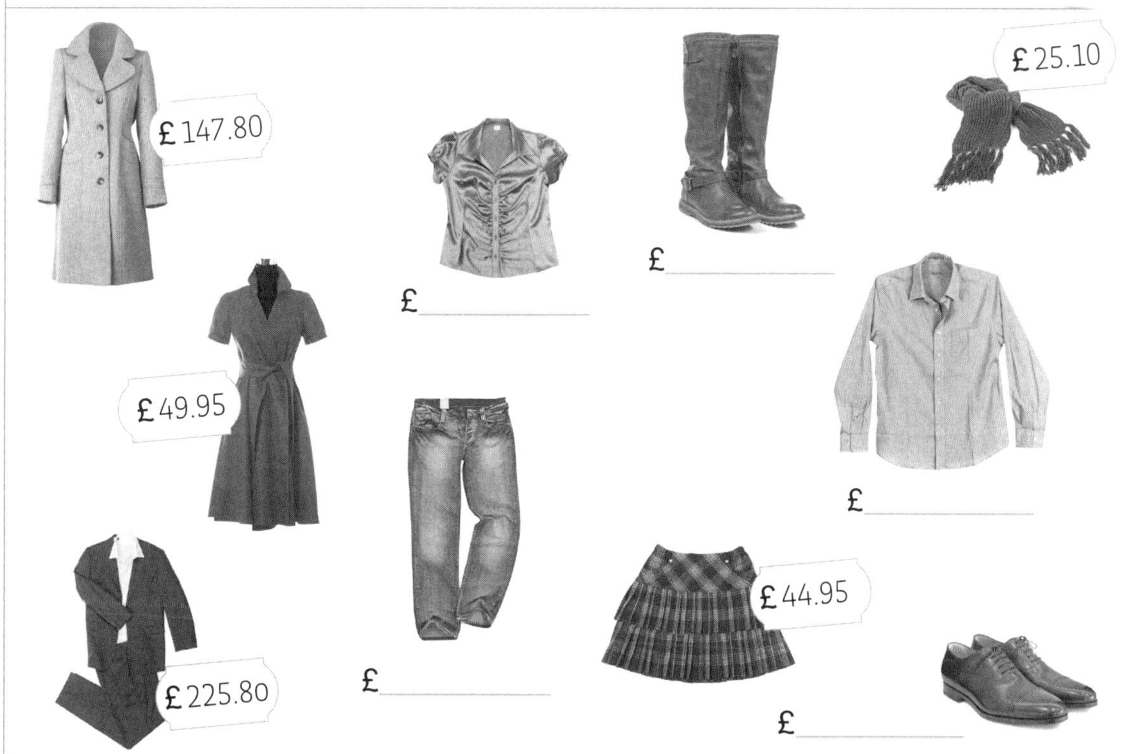

Use Unit 8, after classroom activity 3	**Activity** in pairs; information gap
Duration 15 mins.	**Focus** Saying and understanding the date; Special days around the world

Preparation

Make one copy for each pair of students and cut it in two halves.

Procedure

1. To start the activity, write two or three well-known special days on the board such as *Christmas Day* or *New Year's Eve*. Ask your students: *When's Christmas Day?* Remind them of the difference between writing the date and saying the date. For example, write *25th December* on the board and say *It's on <u>the</u> 25th <u>of</u> December*.
2. Ask students to name a few other special days they know. They can say the days in their mother tongue at this stage, the important thing is for them to understand what we consider a 'special day'.
3. Tell students they are going to ask each other about special days around the world. On their worksheets, some dates are missing. They should ask their partner for the missing dates using the question *When's ...?*
4. Make pairs (Student A and Student B) and hand out the worksheets. Students take turns and ask each other about the dates. They note down the missing dates in the middle column on their worksheet. After students have finished they compare their worksheets in order to see if they wrote the dates correctly.
5. Ask students: *Where do people celebrate Christmas?* (tell them the meaning of *celebrate* if they're not familiar with the word) Elicit some country names. Tell students to work together and think about where the special days on their worksheet are celebrated (the countries are written below the table on their worksheet). Check answers in class by asking, e.g., *Where do people celebrate St. Patrick's Day?*

Extension

As homework each student can look up information about one of the special days from the worksheet on the Internet. The following week, they can briefly tell the class what they found out.

Key

Halloween (31st October): worldwide **St. Patrick's Day** (17th March): Ireland **Groundhog Day** (2nd February): USA **St. Andrew's Day** (30th November): Scotland **Independence Day** (4th July): USA **Buddha's Birthday** (8th April): Japan **Waitangi Day** (6th February): New Zealand **Australia Day** (26th January): Australia **Valentine's Day** (14th February): worldwide **Remembrance Day** (11th November): (mainly) Canada

Student A

Australia | New Zealand | USA (2x) | Canada | Japan | Scotland | Ireland | worldwide (2x)

Special day	When?	Where?
Halloween		
St. Patrick's Day	17th March	
Groundhog Day		
St. Andrew's Day	30th November	
Independence Day		
Buddha's Birthday	8th April	
Waitangi Day		
Australia Day	26th January	
Valentine's Day		
Remembrance Day	11th November	

Student B

Australia | New Zealand | USA (2x) | Canada | Japan | Scotland | Ireland | worldwide (2x)

Special Day	When?	Where?
Halloween	31st October	
St. Patrick's Day		
Groundhog Day	2nd February	
St. Andrew's Day		
Independence Day	4th July	
Buddha's Birthday		
Waitangi Day	6th February	
Australia Day		
Valentine's Day	14th February	
Remembrance Day		

Use Unit 8, after classroom activity 4	**Activity** whole class; miming
Duration 20 mins.	**Focus** Present continuous: positive statements

Preparation

Make one copy of the worksheet and cut up as indicated. You can laminate the cards for future use.

Procedure

1. This miming game can be used to reinforce one of the meanings of the *present continuous* and the active use of the tense. Begin by miming a simple activity such as *playing tennis* and ask your students *What am I doing?* Make sure that students' suggestions are formulated in *present continuous* (*You are playing tennis*). For less confident students, write *You are* (verb)-*ing* on the board as a reminder of the structure.

2. Divide your class into teams of 3, 4 or 5 students (depending on class size). Tell students the different teams are going to mime an activity and the other teams have to guess the activity. The team that first guesses the activity gets a point.

3. Put the paper strips with the activities face down on a desk or a chair and decide which group starts. A student from one of the teams comes up to the class, takes a paper strip from the pile, reads it silently and starts miming the activity. He or she is not allowed to speak. If students think they know the activity they can shout it out.

4. The teams take it in turns to mime activities. For each turn, someone else from the team mimes the activity. The team that first guesses the activity and says it correctly (in *present continuous*) wins a point (keep track of the points on the board for students to see).

5. The team that gets eight points first wins the game.

Variation

If your students are a bit shy, let them 'practice' miming in their groups first. Give two or three activity cards to each group. After a try-out stage students will be more willing to mime in front of the whole class. Also, you and the class can briefly applaud the 'mimes' at the end of their performance.

You are reading a book.	You are drinking a cocktail.
You are doing yoga.	You are playing football.
You are drinking a cup of coffee / tea.	You are swimming.
You are eating spaghetti.	You are playing cards.
You are calling someone from your smartphone.	You are watching TV.
You are driving.	You are listening to pop music.
You are singing in the shower.	You are watching a tennis match.
You are sleeping.	You are playing a computer game.
You are waiting for someone.	You are walking your dog.

Use Unit 9, after classroom activity 4	**Activity** in pairs; information gap
Duration 20 mins.	**Focus** Prepositions of place; Places in a town / city; *Where's …?*

Preparation

Make one copy of the worksheet for each pair of students in your class. Cut up as indicated.

Procedure

1. Start the activity by writing *town* on the top left-hand side of the board and list six locations your students have learned in classroom activity 4, e.g., *bank, church, library, post office, restaurant, cinema*. After that, draw a simple map in the middle of the board: a horizontal street with five boxes above and below it to visualise buildings. Write three locations from your list into the boxes (e.g., *cinema, library, church*).
2. Ask students to imagine they are tourists. Tell them they are looking for the bank, which is not on your map. Elicit the question: *Excuse me, where's the bank?*, and write it on the board. Then answer the question, e.g., *It's next to the library*. Write the answer on the board as well. Then write *bank* into the box next to the library. Encourage students to ask for other buildings (e.g., *post office, restaurant*) and answer their questions using the prepositions they have learned in Unit 9 (*next to, opposite, near,* etc.).
3. Make pairs (Student A and Student B) and hand out the worksheets. Explain to students they are looking for the places in the list at the top of their worksheet. They should take it in turns to ask each other about these places and answer with the information on their map. They should write the name of the place into the correct box.
4. Give students time to get familiar with their map, then start the activity. Monitor during the activity and help individual students if necessary. Note down any common errors or mistakes.
5. After students have finished, they compare their map with their partner's. The two maps should be identical now.
6. If time allows, focus on some common errors that you noted down during the speaking stage. You could write two or three sentences with a gap on the board leaving out the common error, e.g., *The pharmacy is* ______ *Dave's Café*. (*next to / on the left of*)

Extension

If time allows or as homework, students can turn around their map and write as many sentences as they can about the town, for example, *The cinema is opposite the post office*. They should try to do this from memory, without looking back at the map.

Student A

the Marks & Spencer | Luigi's Restaurant | the public library | the Hilton Hotel

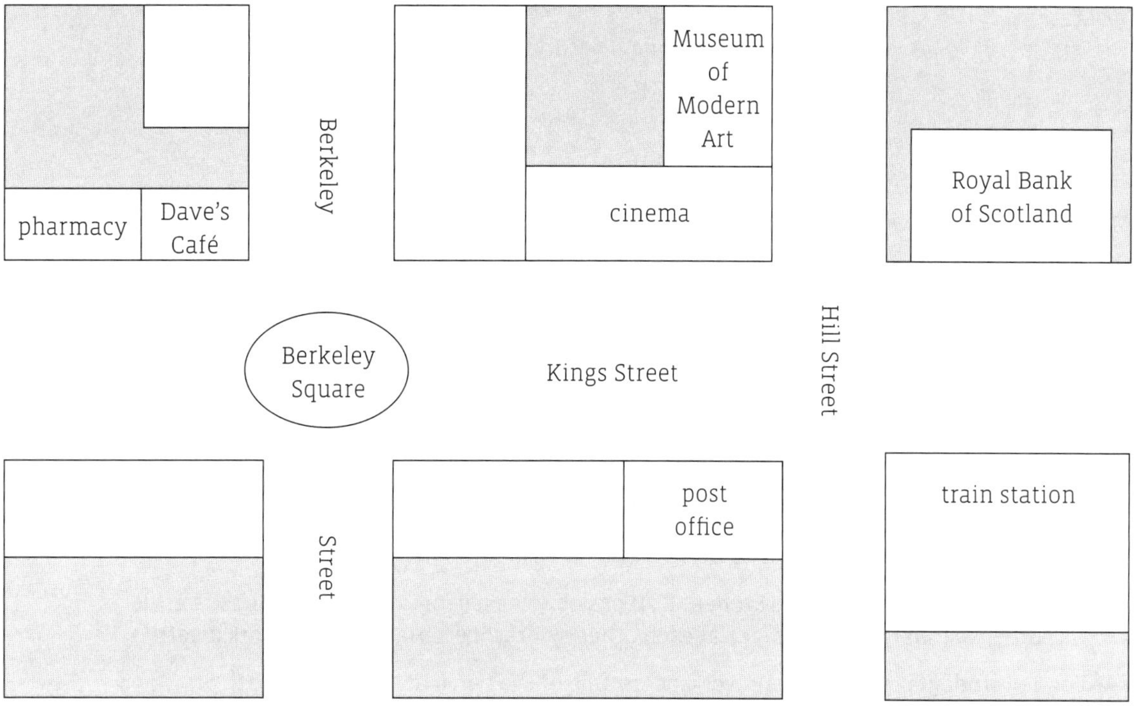

Student B

the post office | the pharmacy | the Royal Bank of Scotland | the Museum of Modern Art

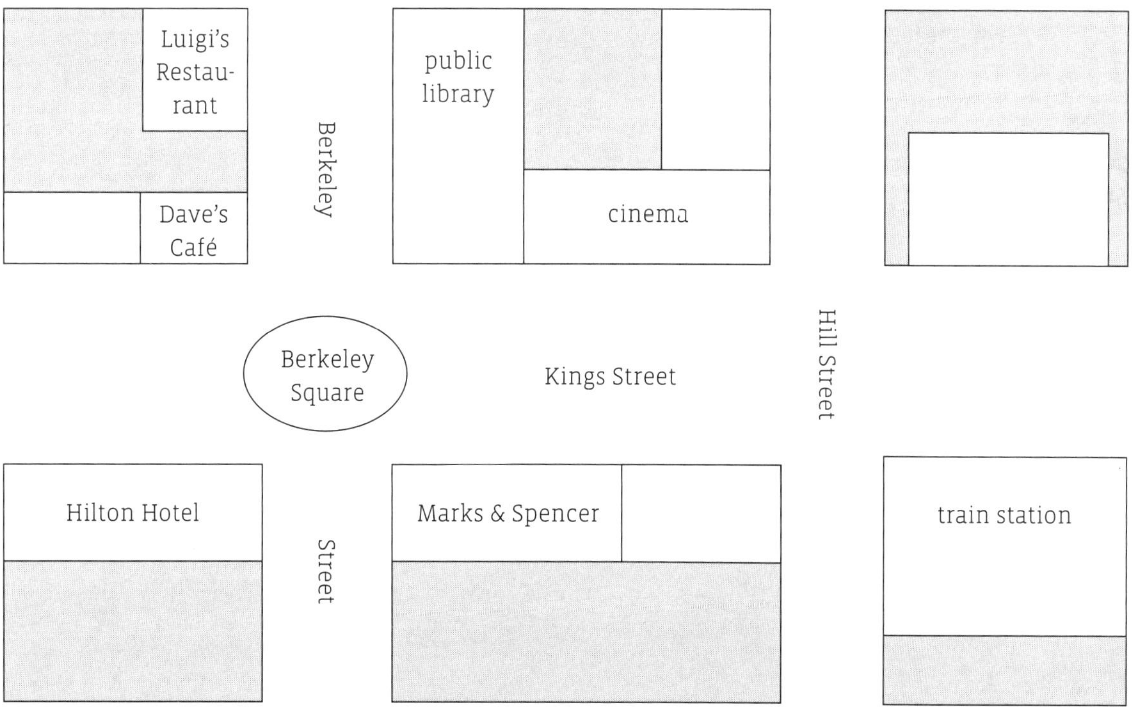

Use Unit 9, after classroom activity 5	**Activity** in pairs; peer dictation
Duration 20 mins.	**Focus** Giving directions; imperative

Preparation

Make one copy of the worksheet for each pair of students in your class. Cut up as indicated.

Procedure

1. If necessary, briefly revise the directions that are needed for the activity. Draw symbols as in classroom activity 5b on the board and elicit the phrases *Turn left. / Turn right. / Go straight on.*
2. After that, draw a dot in the middle of the board and write "You are here" under it. Tell students you are going to draw a line from there. Ask them to give you directions (like the ones you've just revised). After they have given you some instructions, ask them to take you back to your starting point.
3. Make pairs (Student A and Student B). If possible the partners should sit opposite each other so that they cannot look at each other's worksheets. Hand out the worksheets.
4. Tell students to look at their worksheets. One of the two maps on it has a path drawn in, the other one has letters. First, Student A gives Student B directions as the ones just revised, describing the path in the map on their worksheet. Student B follows A's instructions and draws the path from A's worksheet into the map with the letters on their worksheet. Then, it's Student B's turn to give directions and Student A draws the path in their map with the letters.
5. You may want to monitor carefully at this stage of the activity and help if necessary.
6. When students have finished, they should focus on the letters along the line they've drawn. The letters form a sentence.

Key

Student A: The pub is opposite the church.
Student B: It's not far, you can walk.

Student A

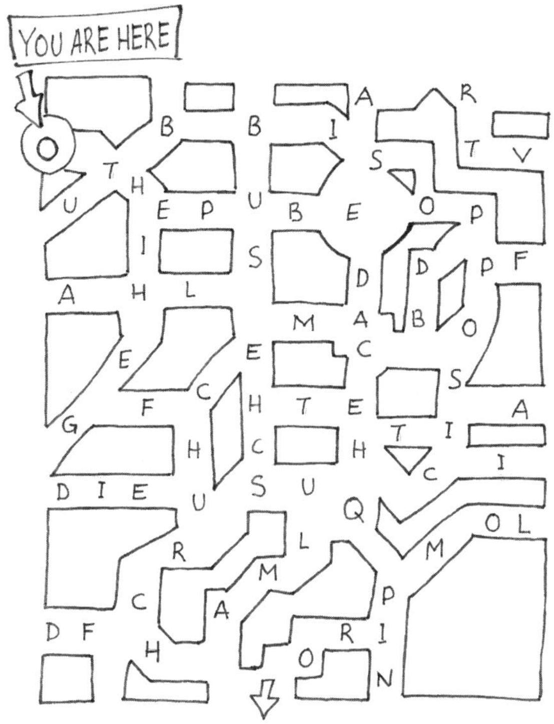

Student B

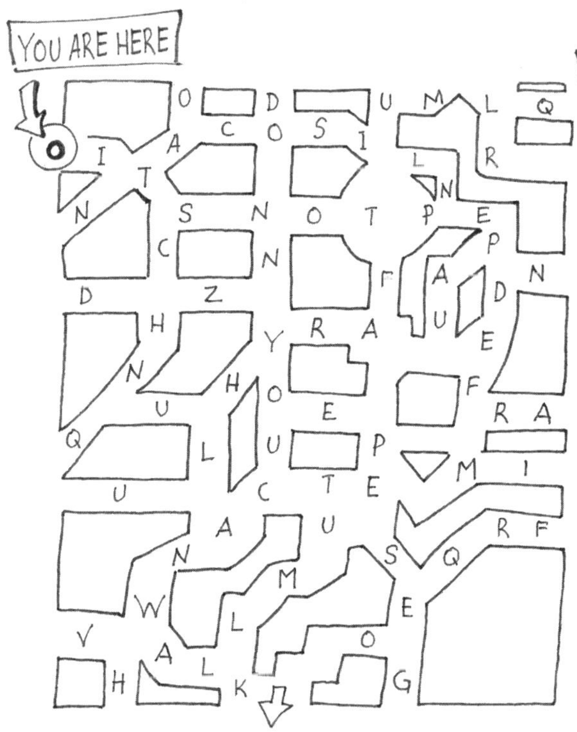

Use Unit 10, after classroom activity 2	**Activity** in groups / pairs; crossword puzzle and information gap
Duration 20 mins.	**Focus** Lexical field: body and health

Preparation

Make one copy of the worksheets for each pair of students in your class. Cut it in two halves.

Procedure

1. The aim of the activity is to complete a crossword puzzle by reading and listening to clues.
2. Divide the students into two groups (Group A and Group B) – make sure there is an equal number of students in each group so that you can pair students up in pairs of two later. Hand out the worksheets (A/B). Tell students to work with their group, read the clues and write the word that is described with the clues into the provided crossword grid.
3. While students are working together in groups, walk around and monitor. Help with vocabulary if necessary.
4. When both groups have finished, write *What's 2 across? / What's 5 down?* on the board. Ask a student from Group A to tell you the clue (but not the solution!) for item 2 across, and a student from Group B to tell you the clue for item 5 down. Tell students they are going to ask each other questions like the ones on the board to complete the crossword.
5. Make pairs with one student from Group A and one student from Group B. Students take it in turns to ask each other questions and read the clues to each other. Encourage students to help their partner with extra clues if they can't find the word with the help of the given clue: they could use gestures or mime the expressions, for example.
6. Start the activity, monitor and help if needed. When students have finished they compare their worksheets. The two crosswords should look the same now.

Key

Across: **2** doctor **6** backache **9** cough **12** painkillers **13** cold **14** fever
Down: **1** stomach ache **3** nose spray **4** healthy **5** pharmacist **7** medicine **8** flu
10 headache **11** massage

Student A

Across:

2 You see this person when you don't feel well. He or she doesn't work in a pharmacy.
9 You have this when you have a cold. It's not a running nose.
14 You have this when your body temperature is higher than normal.

Down:

1 You can get this when you eat a lot of fatty or spicy food.
4 If you eat fresh food and do a lot of sport, you have this kind of lifestyle.
7 You take this when you don't feel well. There are different types, for example syrup, tablets, or nose spray.
10 You have this when your head hurts.

Student B

Across:

6 When you sit for too long and you don't do any sport, you can get this kind of pain.
12 You take them when you have a lot of pain in your body.
13 When you have this, you have a running nose and a cough.

Down:

3 You need this when you have a blocked nose. You can buy it in a pharmacy.
5 This person sells you medicine. He or she can help you when you don't feel well.
8 When you have a headache, a sore throat and a fever then you have this.
11 This helps for back, shoulder or neck pain. It's not a tablet or a cream.

Use Unit 10, after classroom activity 4	**Activity** in pairs; information gap
Duration 30 mins.	**Focus** *How much…?; How many…?; How often…?*

Preparation

Make one copy of the worksheet for each pair of students in your class and cut it in two halves. Prepare two copies of the key below for students to check.

Procedure

1. Ask your students if they like chocolate and if it helps them when they're stressed. Then tell them they are going to read a text about food and a healthy and happy life.

2. Write recommendations for a healthy lifestyle on the board, but leave out some information, e.g., *You should drink … litres of water a day, You should eat … of fish a week, You should eat a fresh salad … a week.* Elicit the questions to ask about the missing information and write them on the board: *How many litres of water should you drink a day?, How much fish should you eat a week?, How often should you eat a fresh salad?*

3. Divide the students into groups (Group A and Group B). There should be an equal number of students in each group so you can make pairs of two later. Hand out the worksheets (A/B). Allow time for students to read the text and help with vocabulary if necessary.

4. Students now write a question for each gap in their text. Refer to the questions on the board for help and encourage students to discuss the questions in their group. When students have finished provide a copy of the key below to each group so students can check if they have written the correct questions.

5. Make pairs with a student from Group A and a student from Group B. Students ask each other their questions and complete the gaps according to their partners' answers. When they have finished, they compare their worksheets (both texts should look the same now).

6. When everybody has finished, have a brief and open class discussion about the text: What do they think about these ideas for a healthy and happy life? Do they agree? Why or why not? Do they have a healthy lifestyle?

Key

(1) How many meals should we eat every day?
(2) How much coffee can you drink a day?
(3) How many glasses of water should you drink a day?
(4) How often a week should you eat a salad with fresh vegetables?
(5) How many carrots do you need for a healthy salad?
(6) How many tomatoes do you need for a healthy salad?
(7) How often can you eat cheese and yoghurt?
(8) How much pasta and rice can you eat a week?
(9) How much meat a month is enough?
(10) How many pieces of chocolate a day are enough?

Student A

Does chocolate make you happy?

Many people today have a stressful life, and they eat bad food. This is not only unhealthy – it also makes you unhappy, says Dr Carl Joy, a specialist for a happy life.

Healthy food is on Dr Joy's hit list for a happier life. He says we should eat ______________ **(1)** meals every day. A breakfast with muesli and fresh fruit is a good start into a happy day. You can drink two cups **(2)** of coffee a day – but not more! Water is a lot better for you, says Dr Joy – you should drink at least ______________ **(3)** glasses a day.

Fresh food is also important. You should eat a salad with fresh vegetables three times a week **(4)** – this brings energy to your body and helps you when you are stressed and tired.

For a healthy salad, you only need some lettuce, ______________ **(5)** carrots and five **(6)** tomatoes.

You can eat cheese and yoghurt ______________ **(7)**, but be careful with the fat – it makes you tired. Pasta and rice are good for your energy levels – you can eat five kilograms **(8)** a week. Meat is not on Dr Joy's hit list for a happy life – ______________ **(9)** of meat a month is enough! And in general, chicken is better for you than pork.

What about chocolate? Does it really make us happy? Dr Joy says it does – chocolate helps you to relax and to feel good. But three **(10)** pieces of chocolate a day are enough. Good to know. So enjoy your life and don't forget: Don't worry – be happy!

✂ -

Student B

Does chocolate make you happy?

Many people today have a stressful life, and they eat bad food. This is not only unhealthy – it also makes you unhappy, says Dr Carl Joy, a specialist for a happy life.

Healthy food is on Dr Joy's hit list for a happier life. He says we should eat three **(1)** meals every day. A breakfast with muesli and fresh fruit is a good start into a happy day. You can drink ______________ **(2)** of coffee a day – but not more! Water is a lot better for you, says Dr Joy – you should drink at least six **(3)** glasses a day.

Fresh food is also important. You should eat a salad with fresh vegetables ______________ **(4)** – this brings energy to your body and helps you when you are stressed and tired.

For a healthy salad, you only need some lettuce, three **(5)** carrots and ______________ **(6)** tomatoes.

You can eat cheese and yoghurt every day **(7)**, but be careful with the fat – it makes you tired. Pasta and rice are good for your energy levels – you can eat ______________ **(8)** a week. Meat is not on Dr Joy's hit list for a happy life – one kilogram **(9)** of meat a month is enough! And in general, chicken is better for you than pork.

What about chocolate? Does it really make us happy? Dr Joy says it does – chocolate helps you to relax and to feel good. But ______________ **(10)** pieces of chocolate a day are enough. Good to know. So enjoy your life and don't forget: Don't worry – be happy!

Use	Activity
Unit 11, after classroom activity 3	in pairs; role play
Duration	**Focus**
30 mins.	Asking for information about an event; *can; have to*

Preparation

Make one copy of the two worksheets for each pair of students in your class. Prepare some copies of the key below for students to check.

Procedure

1. Tell your students they are going to ask for information about upcoming events in New York and London. Their partner will be the ticket seller and will answer their questions about the event.
2. Make pairs (Student A and Student B). Hand out the worksheets. Tell students to first think about and write down questions they can ask about an upcoming event. They can do this on their own or in pairs, and they can look at the ideas at the top of the worksheet for help. If they do this with their partner, they shouldn't show them the lower half of the worksheet. When students have finished, you can provide copies of the key so students can check if they have written the questions correctly.
3. Next, ask students to look at the poster on the lower half of their worksheet. Ask them to find the information they need to answer the questions they have written down. Allow enough time for this.
4. Now students practice dialogues at a ticket office: First, Student A is the client and asks Student B, the ticket seller, questions about an upcoming event in London. Student B answers with the information from their event poster. Then, Student B is the client and asks A about an event in New York. A answers as the ticket seller (with the information from their poster). Encourage the ticket sellers to sound friendly as they are pretending to be at a ticket office.
5. You may want to walk around and monitor carefully during the speaking stage. Help only if absolutely necessary as this is supposed to be a fluency activity.
6. If time allows, hold a brief class feedback: What did students find difficult or easy and why? Answer any questions that students might have.

Key

(possible questions) Is there an interesting event this weekend? / Do you still have tickets? / Do I/we have to reserve tickets? / When does it start? / When do I/we have to be there? / How much are the tickets? / Is there a discount?

Student A

You want to go out in London. Write questions you can ask the ticket seller.

- interesting event this weekend?
- still have tickets?
- have to reserve tickets?
- when / start?
- when / be there?
- how much / tickets?
- discount?

You are a ticket seller in New York. Think about how you can answer your client's questions. Think of answers to the questions above.

New York Jazz Festival

Famous jazz musicians from all over the country play their favourite songs in your city!

Where: The Cotton Club

When: Friday, 24th to Sunday 26th
always from 7 p.m. to midnight
Please arrive half an hour before opening.

Tickets:
Friday: sold out; Saturday and Sunday: still available
Reserve online
For one night – $45 per person
For three nights – $120 per person
(no discount)

Payment: Credit card or cash

Student B

You want to go out in New York. Write questions you can ask the ticket seller.

- interesting event this weekend?

- still have tickets?

- have to reserve tickets?

- when / start?

- when / be there?

- how much / tickets?

- discount?

You are a ticket seller in London. Think about how you can answer your client's questions.
Think of answers to the questions above.

Poetry Slam!

Young writers perform their texts in the theatre.
You decide who is the best performer of the night!

Where: Soho Theatre Company

When: Saturday, 12th
Doors open at 8 p.m.
(Be there 20 minutes earlier!)

Tickets:
Available: reserve by phone or buy at the door
£10,50 per person
(With student discount: £7,50)

Payment: Cash only (at ticket office)

Use Unit 11, after classroom activity 4	Activity whole class; mingling
Duration 20 mins.	**Focus** Making arrangements; Present continuous for fixed plans and arrangements

Preparation

Make a copy of the worksheet for each pair of students in your class. Cut it in two halves.

Procedure

1. As a lead-in, ask your students about their plans for the following day: *What are you doing tomorrow evening?* Make sure they use the *present continuous* in their responses. Then tell students they are going to plan their next week's free time activities together with the other students in the class. Revise the language of making arrangements (introduced in classroom activity 3) and write it on the board. Make sure to include an initial question, possible responses, a suggestion for a free-time activity and a positive reaction to it (see boardscript).

■ Are you free on Friday evening?	
● Sure, I'm free on Friday evening. ■ Let's go to the cinema. ● That sounds great!	● Sorry, I'm busy on Friday evening. I'm doing yoga. What about Saturday? ■ Sure, I'm free on Saturday afternoon. Let's go to the cinema. ● That sounds great!

2. Hand out the worksheets. Ask students to choose seven activities from the list at the top of their worksheet or to use their own ideas, and write them in the diary.

3. When students have written down the activities, they get up and walk around the class with their worksheet. They talk to other students and make seven more arrangements that they note down in their diary. If they're busy on a specific day, they need to say why and suggest an alternative date.

4. In the reporting stage, students should not only say <u>what</u> they are doing on a given day but also <u>who</u> they are doing it with, e.g., *I'm going to a concert with Tanja on Monday evening.* If time allows, hold a brief class feedback or spend some time on common errors you noticed during the speaking stage of the activity.

Variation

With less than six students, it's best if students work in pairs or in groups of 3. They should make seven arrangements with their partner or team. Initiate a brief reporting stage by asking, e.g., *Timo, Lisa and Christoph, what are you doing on Monday afternoon?*

Student A

do yoga | go to a birthday party | go swimming | go to a musical / concert | go shopping
go to the theatre / to the cinema | go to an art gallery | have a massage
have dinner with a friend | have coffee with a colleague | meet friends for drinks

	Monday	Tuesday	Wednesday	Thursday	Friday	Saturday	Sunday
afternoon							
evening							

✂ -

Student B

do yoga | go to a birthday party | go swimming | go to a musical / concert | go shopping
go to the theatre / cinema | go to an art gallery | have a massage
have dinner with a friend | have coffee with a colleague | meet friends for drinks

	Monday	Tuesday	Wednesday	Thursday	Friday	Saturday	Sunday
afternoon							
evening							

Use Unit 12, after classroom activity 2	Activity in pairs; puzzle and information gap
Duration 20 mins.	**Focus** Talking about personal information and language skills

Preparation

Make one copy of the worksheet for each pair of students in your class. Cut it in two halves.

Procedure

1. Show students the worksheet and tell them they are going to solve a puzzle and find out more about four people living in four different houses on the same street.
2. Elicit the questions students will need for the activity: Ask them how to ask (a) where someone's from, (b) what their job is, (c) what languages they speak, and (d) what languages they'd like to learn. Introduce the question *Who lives in house (3)?* since students will have to ask for the names of certain neighbours. Write the questions on the board as a reference.
3. Make groups (Group A and Group B) and hand out the worksheets. First, ask students to read the sentences below the table. With this information, they should be able to fill in some (but not all!) cells of the table: each student should fill in ten cells. They should read the sentences carefully and then re-read them so they don't miss anything. If they have trouble finding the solutions, they should ask someone from their group for help.
4. After that, students find a partner from the other group. They should use the questions you've written on the board to ask their partner for the missing information. While they're doing this, walk around, listen in and note down common errors.
5. When students have finished, they compare their tables (which should look the same now), or you can check solutions in class by asking questions, e.g., *Where is Andrew from?* If time allows, have a short error correction stage.

Key

	House 1:	House 2:	House 3:	House 4:
Name	Paulina	Andrew	Alice	Boris
Job	designer	English teacher	artist	retired
From	Columbia	Scotland	Australia	Russia
Speaks	English, Spanish, Portuguese	English, Italian	English	English, Russian, French
Would like to learn	Italian	Chinese	Spanish	German

Student A

	House 1	House 2	House 3	House 4
Name			Alice	
Job				
Country				
Speaks				
Would like to learn				

The English teacher is from Scotland.

The man who lives next to Alice is from Russia.

Alice is an artist. She's from Australia and she only speaks English.

One of the women in the street is fluent in English, Spanish and Portuguese.

The woman from house number 1 is a designer. Her neighbour is an English teacher.

One of Alice's neighbours is retired. He's fluent in English and Russian, and he speaks a bit of French.

Student B

	House 1	House 2	House 3	House 4
Name	Paulina			
Job				
Country				
Speaks				
Would like to learn				

Andrew would like to learn Chinese.

Boris lives in house 4. He wants to learn German.

Paulina is from Columbia. She would like to learn Italian.

The man who would like to learn Chinese speaks two languages: Italian and English.

The woman in the house next to Boris is an artist. She only speaks English but she would like to learn Spanish.

Use	Activity
Unit 12, after classroom activity 4	in pairs; interview and quiz
Duration	**Focus**
40 mins.	Theory of Multiple Intelligences (H. Gardner); *like + -ing* (revision); *Are you good at...?*

Preparation

Make a copy of the worksheet for each student in your class. Bring three bigger pictures of famous people (see suggestions below) to show in class.

Procedure

1. This activity introduces students to Howard Gardner's theory of "Multiple Intelligences" and the idea that everybody learns differently. The activities on the worksheet help students to reflect what their strengths and weaknesses are and how they learn best.
2. As a lead-in, show students three pictures of famous people, for example Albert Einstein, Michael Jackson and William Shakespeare. Ask students if they think that these people are smart. Also ask them what these people are good at. Introduce the adjective *smart* (as a synonym for *intelligent*) and the structure *to be good at + -ing*. Write both on the board.
3. Tell your students briefly about Howard Gardner's theory, according to which everybody is smart (intelligent), but that we can be smart in (at least eight) different ways. No one has only one type of intelligence, but each type may be more or less strong in a person. Someone like Albert Einstein can be considered mostly 'logic smart' ("mathematical intelligence" according to Howard Gardner), whereas Michael Jackson was rather 'music smart' ("musical-rhythmic intelligence") and William Shakespeare 'word smart' ("verbal-linguistic intelligence").
4. Next, students should think about their own strengths. Ask: *What are you good at*?, and hand out a worksheet to each student. Students start by reading through the questions at the top and ticking the boxes next to them if they can answer with a 'yes'. Then, they interview a partner and tick the boxes on the right.
5. Students read through the definitions on the lower half of the worksheet and match each way of being smart with its definition. Compare answers in class.
6. Finally, ask students in what ways they think they are smart. The upside-down solutions at the bottom of the page show which questions from the interview at the top point to which type of intelligence. Then hold a brief class feedback. What are students' main strengths? Did their partner have a different result? What is a good learning strategy for a person who is, for example, word smart or logic smart? You may want to hold the class feedback in student's mother tongue to keep the discussion light and easy to follow.

Extension

If students find the theory interesting, they can look up "Multiple Intelligences" ('Multiple Intelligenzen') on the Internet and learn more about Howard Gardner's ideas.

Tick ✓ what's true for you. Then interview a partner and tick what's true for him or her.

question	me	my partner
1. Do you like singing?		
2. Do you like telling stories?		
3. Do you like taking photos?		
4. Do you like playing Sudoku?		
5. Do you like helping your friends?		
6. Do you know a lot about animals?		
7. Do you like thinking about yourself?		
8. Are you good at finding streets on a map?		
9. Do you like making things with your hands?		
10. Do you often talk with friends on the phone?		
11. Do you like studying English alone at home?		
12. Do you like going for a walk in the countryside?		
13. When you went to school, were you good at maths?		
14. Do you like reading books, newspapers and magazines?		
15. Are you good at playing basketball, football or doing yoga?		
16. Do you like listening to music when you work or study English?		

Match the ways of being smart on the left with the definitions on the right.

music smart	You like working with photos or pictures. You are good at explaining the way and giving directions.
word smart	You like working alone. You like thinking. You know yourself very well.
body smart	You enjoy working with other people in a team. You are good at talking to people. You like discussions.
logic smart	You like learning about nature. You know the names of many animals, trees and flowers.
self smart	You find it easy to learn languages. You are good at reading and writing. You like telling stories.
people smart	You like to move. You are good at sports and/or dancing. You like making things with your hands.
picture smart	You like singing and listening to music. Maybe you play an instrument.
nature smart	You like numbers. You are good at maths. You enjoy logical puzzles and quizzes.

Solutions: music smart (1; 16) body smart (9; 15) self smart (7; 11) picture smart (3; 8)
word smart (2; 14) logic smart (4; 13) people smart (5; 10) nature smart (6; 12)